TWELVE
Slanted
POEMS FOR CHRISTMAS
Edited by Helen Ivory & Kate Birch

Tell all the Truth but tell it slant -
Emily Dickinson

ink
sweat
&tears
PRESS

Published by Ink Sweat & Tears Press
London SW12 8DG
inksweatandtears.co.uk

Introduction and selection © Helen Ivory & Kate Birch
Copyright of poems rests with the authors.
Design: Nick Stone, Starfish Limited
Cover image © Helen Ivory
helenivory.co.uk
Photo courtesy of Martin Figura
Typeset 10pt on 12.5pt Sabon Roman
Printed and bound by Swallowtail Print, Norwich.

ISBN 978-0-9927253-0-3

Introduction

Since 2007, UK based webzine *Ink Sweat & Tears* has been publishing and reviewing poetry, prose, prose-poetry, word & image pieces and everything in between.

TWELVE has been inspired by *IS&T*'s annual 'Twelve Days of Christmas' feature where we issue a general invite to submit works with a Christmas connection. What has always struck us about the variety of excellent submissions we receive is that they inevitably embody a skewed response to the season. So we decided to approach a group of leading contemporary UK poets whom we very much admired for their slanted viewpoint with the idea of putting together a festive volume of shiny new poems.

Now let us present to you . . . contemporary scenes of domestic gothic; of family tenderness and detachment; of a green jelly tsunami engulfing a tinseled high street. It snows, bankers gorge on chocolate coins and the Salvation Army fights to play in time. This is not the advertised Christmas.

We hope this will be the first of many *IS&T Slanted* anthologies.

Contents

Factory Spirit

Tell your dad you are close to the beautiful
poem, living in a makeshift moon, running from evil
pictures. Don't compare prescription drugs
to a mother's hug or a daydream made of paper,
that will only make him angry. Let him think
you're stoned again, staring at your dirty feet
on the grass, wondering how to make him laugh
before it's too late for the tumbling sky
and his thin, white hair. He talks about the phantom
smell of wartime pipe-smoke on his night shift.
How he desperately longs to see the factory spirit,
to know there's something else before
they lay him off again. He'd like to see his mother.
He taps the table with a silver lighter, squints
at clouds that look like Christmas ghosts.
A robin on your neighbour's fence is holding
a small crucifix in its beak. Your dad sees it too,
but he doesn't say anything. You tell him sometimes
you wish you were a ghost, so that you could make him happy.
He sighs because the world is a headache; he doesn't know
what happened. He tells you that he drifts through the old
buildings every night, talking to the dark, until it's time
to go home. And for some reason it reminds you
of love. I mean it seems like your dad is talking
about love. And for a few seconds you can't remember
very much about your life, as you push your toes
under the cool soil and realise his lucky silver lighter
is broken, and that is why he isn't smoking.

Bobby Parker

Masterchristmas

This Christmas, I miss us. On the speaker
I can hear your voice. In both ears. You are not here
for me to say in person you're precious. You know

how time goes: when you're grown, there is nothing new
on Christmas morning, in the fancy packaging,
asking questions of what others think of us.

Did you like what you got? It's only half my gift.
The rest is going to be home cooking. Put your ingredients,
now, up on the counter. Start the camera. Let's *begin*. I'll do

the work: if you have, correctly, placed the veg, and the protein,
in order - right there. Thanks to the wonder of science,
I slip on cybergloves. My hands move where you are.

So much perfect togetherness
across the world and, viewer, I'm its chef. Your kitchen,
the same as my one, remote-controlling, replicating love.

Hail the supreme ruler of us all. Every Christmas house
should be identical to this, if you put your ingredients
now, up on the counter, start the camera, and we *begin*. I'll do

the work: if you have, correctly, placed the veg, and the protein,
in order - right there. Thanks to the wonder of science,
I slip on cybergloves. My hands move where you are.

Ira Lightman

Winter

is its own lonely scarab
no one doubts it
as cold days
lengthen
into winter-april
sheepfarm hours
snow cities drifting
along their frozen rivers
in the different light
of climate shock
dolomite air
falling smack
on to thin roofs
skyfall days
bound in ice
nights a-quail
a comet lashes
its fiery tail
too far away
to warm us
who live in one room
too poor
thanks to the bad banks
to heat the rest of the house

Penelope Shuttle

Broken

At Christmas Sun Daddy started smashing glass

he started in his bedroom,
then swept tornado-like through the house:

windows, ornaments, glass lampshades,
the rented TV – nothing was safe.

When things quietened down,
they found him with his head on the kitchen table.

The room glittered around him.

Julia Webb

Watch

Like my Dad, my Christmas job, it seems,
is balling wrapping paper into bags.

You tear through plastic things you'll soon forget
until one more, held back 'til last, a watch.

We sit together, watching seconds tick,
Wow, Dad, you say, *it's going really fast.*

Luke Wright

Angels

They fold their wings
over the wings of the house.
Over the Dementia Wing.

On Christmas morning the manager
wears a diaphanous dress and exclaims
How lovely it is
that so many of the residents
are being taken out today. But it's hard
if they don't know why they're there –
and might not want to go back.

Angels are needed to smooth their passage,
help them into cars. An old man
smiles his broadest smile
at the Carer in royal blue.
My angel he says, *you're my angel!*
She copes with him –
and her recent divorce. Most days

she has more medicines to issue
than Santa has presents in his sack.
The medicine trolley – it trundles along.
Those white boxes of pills.
That snow-clad city.

Moniza Alvi

Finishing *The Mill on the Floss* on Christmas Eve

> *...the wide area of watery desolation...spread out in dreadful clearness...*

The brother and sister, no sooner reunited—

> *... in dreadful clearness floated onward the hurrying, threatening...*

—than the flood waters came, bearing—

> *..."It is coming, Maggie!" Tom said, in a...*

—death.

> *...deep, hoarse voice, loosing the oars, and clasping her....*

Minutes, I suppose, later, I raised my wet face,
blinked to sharpen the blurry
kaleidoscope of colour and form.

I drifted downstairs. On the dining table, gold
and red bows; clear tape; scissors; long rolls
and odd scraps of wrapping paper printed
with snowmen, candy canes, reindeer.

Stepping into the living room, I saw my mother
place presents beneath the branches.
I stared into the twinkling lights, and the colours
blurred and shifted under the pressure.

I blinked to see her distinct.
I stood watching, devastated and whole.

Carrie Etter

In The Bleak Midwinter

At the ragged edge of the old year, when the dead
Thorn-spiked branches thrashed in the wind, I lived in a tree.
How I came there hardly matters, money was never a
Overwhelming need. Still, I was tired and cold,
My feet in trainers and one pair of socks. Such a
Elongated stay outdoors rotted my nails. Back in Fall
A red fox led me here; hollow cemetery yew I
Made into a home among the grave-stones. A shiv
Of ice broken from branch quenched thirst, a fire
Negotiated with moss gave warmth. I had a
Great anthology, poetry, a Bible, a lung
That ached with infection. I know that you were born, a
Human being, in May or June. This was the time I
Etched out to understand your word: Resurrection.

Bethany W Pope

Spent

The days before that late day in December
are the dreadful tunings of instruments.
It is all sleep in the eyes and glitter

as the Salvation Army plays the sombre
ragged tunes of afternoon on Christmas
Eve, outside the shops.

The green but cruel holly holds berries
to task, as if in their redness they might
stave the squalor of money changing

hands, or distract from the tinsel's
tatty smile over the tills. The door to the precinct
slows as it closes the cold to the night.

Little reindeer dance in silence and light
over the entrance. The car park is cheap after 3
and the ashtray on the wall is swollen with kissed cigarettes.

This is the flimsy set of Christmas to be taken down,
if not by snow, then cold hands tired of *tidings
of comfort and joy*, foil bows and receipts.

The fruit we eat has come a long way.

Andrea Holland

Room at the Inn

Three Boxing Days in a row, scurrying across the Valley Bridge –
and this long before they put up screens to stop
the seasonal depressive lemming-fest, which they had said
couldn't be done, budgetary constraints, aesthetic considerations
&c., until that bloke went over with his kiddies in his arms,
and then suddenly wasn't the cash found sharp enough –
to open up, because there are barbarians, and thirsty ones at that,
outside the citadel, who have not seen the inside of a bar
these two dozen hours now, and have endured the soft hum
of familial small talk and drunk only in moderation,
and must now be watered like rosetted livestock,
for do they not put bread upon the table of the licensed victualer class,
and will be, even now, battering on the door as sweat drips down
your sleeve, overcoat collar chafes your neck, and yes, for the third
consecutive year, in too-short eighties shorts, comes loping past,
candy-floss hair billowing, the über-creep, the Tories' chum,
James Wilson Vincent Savile; and it's a small thing to hate him for,
we all agree, tapping glasses in fraternal salutation, but it's a start.

Tim Turnbull

Mother Goo

McGueegueg smoothed the lacquered sneer of his quiff
and slid a harpoon-like forearm along the seatback,
rippling the russet leather billows of his Ford Peyote.
Ron Maelstrom shrugged it off, not having been driven in
to a showing of 20,000 Leagues for this. Half-turning
in protest, he took in the green jelly tsunami which quivered
behind them, police cars pulsing in its bio-luminescent maw,
and permitted himself a single elongated squeak.
Steve sneaked out the parking lot while Mother dined.
Since Chief Ernest Borg had been assimilated, who
would lead the town? Running down its tinsellated drag,
waving in a frenzy at the friendly uninitiated shoppers,
he crashed into Captain Rehab, the bear-hearted rogue
who had, during long spells in the state asylum, inscribed
scenes from his inner voyages upon his own incisors,
which he bared now, thirstlessly and stinking of myrrh:
'Stevie boy, what's your hurry? Don't you like me?'
McQueegueg indicated the now aurora-large bulbous invader,
nine splay-limbed consumers hanging in her midst
as in a macedoine, emitting a perfume of macerated cake.
Immediately Rehab drew his Magnum and took aim:
there were a series of luckless punks as the shells hit home –
though one took out a partially digested Baptist.
'She doesn't mind the perforations,' Steve explained
as they reversed a 4 x 4 before her avenue-devouring mass.

Meanwhile, excreted onto a parkbench and inexplicably
wearing his neighbour's kimono, blinged with gunk,
Maelstrom vomited Goo's innards in the bin, noting
they went down in a spiral like a foie gras galaxy.
His mind was brilliantly cleared, as though nano-Buddha
had gone through it with a nailbrush, leaving nada.
Around him, like freshly laundered zombies, townsfolk
with more or less all their limbs and faces, lurched
toward their houses, emptied of Christmas but left
with its spirit, far too neat. He watched the space-saliva
race like green mercury about his limbs before finding
an orifice and slipping in. He was totally wormed.
In the drained fountain was a banjo, fashioned from
the shell of a sea turtle, still warm from the tuning:
he strummed it and sang the shanties of that species
which will follow us down Mother's universal gullet.

WN Herbert

The Norwich Version

After the dancing ladies and their ever-leaping lords
Christmas ran out of music, lost its melodies and chords,
its rhythm was shot to pieces, despite the piping pipes
of which there were eleven of various sundry types,
and it would be disaster, for we all knew what was coming
until there suddenly appeared a dozen drummers drumming.

A dozen drummers drumming followed by eight maids
each of them on with milking pails, with stools and udder aids,
with seven stately swans in tow, elderly and greying,
six highly fattened pregnant geese copiously laying,
five gold rings, four colly birds, three lah-di-dah French hens
two turtle doves, some pigeons, one and three-quarter wrens

so when the music was restored and fit to make a sonnet
there was just a pear tree left with Alan Partridge on it.

George Szirtes

Helen Ivory has published four collections of poetry, her latest being *Waiting for Bluebeard* (Bloodaxe, May 2013). She is co-editor with George Szirtes of *In their Own Words: Contemporary Poets on their Poetry* (Salt, 2012). In addition to editing *IS&T*, she has over twelve years teaching experience including for the Arvon Foundation and the Poetry School.

Kate Birch has spent most of her adult life writing about subjects as varied as 18th Century politics, machine tools and tap dancing. She works behind the scenes at *IS&T*.